DATE DUE	MAR 0 7		
GAYLORD			PRINTED IN U.S.A.

Stick Insect

Diane A. Kelly

KIDHAVEN PRESS

An imprint of Thomson Gale, a part of The Thomson Corporation

Detroit • ... • London • Munich

For more information, contact
Kidhaven Press
27500 Drake Rd.
Farmington Hills, MI 48331-3535
Or you can visit our Internet site at http://www.gale.com

LIBRARY OF CONGRESS CATALOGING-IN-PUBLICATION DATA

Kelly, Diane A.
  Stick Insect / by Diane A. Kelly.
    p. cm. — (Bugs)
Includes bibliographical references and index.
Summary: Describes the physical characteristics of stick insects, their life cycle, where they live, and their eating habits.
  ISBN 0-7377-1774-2 (hardback : alk. paper)
  1. Stick insect—Juvenile literature. [1. Stick insect.] I. Title. II. Series.

Printed in China

CONTENTS

Masters of Disguise

Stick insects are hard to see. People can look right at one without noticing it because a stick insect does not look like a typical insect at all. It looks like part of a stick or a branch.

Scientists call stick insects **phasmids**. They are found all over the world, but most kinds live in the tropics of Central America, South America, and Asia.

Opposite: This magnified image shows a stick insect's eyes, mouthparts, and antennae.

A tropical walkingstick blends in with its surroundings to hide from predators.

There are twenty-four species of stick insects in the United States. Here they are commonly called walkingsticks, devil's horses, or prairie alligators.

Stick insects are bigger than most bugs. Most are between one and four inches long, but a few get even larger. The longest stick insect in North America is six inches long. And that seems small compared to the giant walkingstick from Southeast Asia, which can grow to more than twenty inches long. That is longer than some newborn human babies!

Stick Insect Bodies

Like all insects, stick insects have bodies divided into three parts. They have a head, a **thorax**, and an **abdomen**. Each of these parts helps hide, or **camouflage**, the stick insect from **predators**.

The short head contains two of the stick insect's sense organs: the eyes and the **antennae**. Their eyes are small and found on the sides of the head. The antennae, which are used for smelling, look like long, thin threads.

The middle of the stick insect's body is called the thorax. It is very long, as are the six thin legs that attach here. The front two legs have notches at their bases that match the shape of the stick insect's head. When the stick insect is resting, it can hide its head between the notches to make itself look more like a twig. It can also point each of its other legs in a different direction to make itself look like a twig with many branches.

Some stick insects have no wings. Others have two pairs of short wings attached to the thorax. Only the hind wings are used for flying.

A stick insect points its front legs upward (far left) to make itself look like a twig.

Body of a Stick Insect

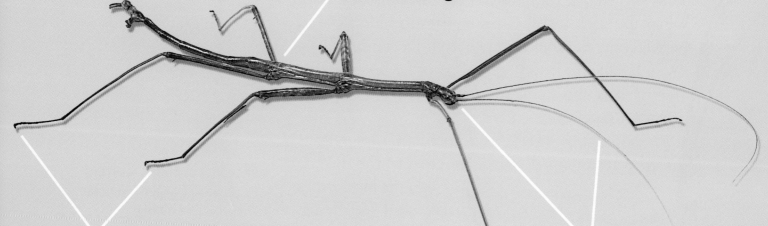

Hard exoskeleton protects the insect's soft insides, and helps the insect blend in with its surroundings.

Six long legs can be pointed in different directions, giving the insect its stick-like appearance.

Two small eyes and two long antennae act as the insect's sense organs.

The front pair, called **tegmina**, are leathery. They cover and protect the delicate hind wings when the stick insect is resting. When the insect flies, it holds the tegmina out of the way.

The last part of the body is the abdomen. Like the thorax, it is long and thin and looks like a stick.

Like all insects, stick insects are covered by a hard **exoskeleton**. This covering supports and protects the soft muscles and organs. The exoskeleton is usually green or brown. This coloring helps the stick insect blend in with leaves and branches. Sometimes they have spots that look like mold or bird droppings. Other stick insects can change color to match their surroundings.

Some stick insects have exoskeletons with bumps and projections that look like thorns or partly eaten leaves. Bumps on the thorax, legs, or abdomen help the insect look more like a plant. Other stick insects have ridges on their exoskeleton that make them look like bark. The moss insect from Central America has so many small points sticking off its exoskeleton that it looks just like a piece of moss.

CHAPTER

2

Life Cycle

Opposite: Stick insects mate on the surface of a leaf. After mating, the female lays hundreds of eggs, like this one shown magnified (inset).

Although stick insects can live for more than a year, the adults live only long enough to mate and lay eggs. When a female stick insect is ready to mate, she releases a chemical called a **pheromone**. A male stick insect can smell this chemical from very far away and will hurry to find the female. After he finds her, he will ride on her back for days or even weeks to keep other males away. After mating, the male dies.

A thorny phasmid nymph rests on a leaf shortly after hatching.

A female stick insect lays hundreds of eggs. Some kinds of stick insects drop the eggs onto the ground or hide them in cracks in tree bark. Others bury them in the soil or glue them to leaves and stems. After she produces her eggs, she dies.

In the Egg

Because female stick insects die after laying their eggs, they cannot guard them. So they camouflage their eggs with hard shells that look like plant seeds. Some kinds of stick insects add a fatty structure called a **capitulum** to one end of their eggs. The capitulum attracts ants, which carry the egg into their nest. The ants eat the capitulum and then throw the egg unharmed onto their trash heap. The egg stays safely underground until it hatches, protected from weather, predators, and other threats.

One of these other threats is the cleptis wasp. The cleptis wasp is a parasite. When a female wasp finds a stick insect egg, she lays her own eggs inside it. When the wasp larvae hatch, they eat the baby stick insect alive inside the egg.

Stick insect eggs can take a long time to hatch. Many do not hatch for over a year. Some eggs take as long as two years. When a stick insect finally hatches, it exits through a trap door at one end of the egg. The trap door is called the **operculum**. The stick insect **nymph** pushes the operculum off the egg with its head. It then climbs up the nearest plant and starts eating.

Growing Up

Stick insect nymphs look like tiny adults except they do not have wings. These develop later. Like the adults, the nymphs have an exoskeleton. But the exoskeleton cannot grow. So the nymphs must shed it, or **molt**, as they grow.

Molting can be dangerous for stick insect nymphs. During a molt, a nymph puffs itself up with air until its exoskeleton splits along the center of its back. Then it carefully climbs out of its old skeleton. Because its legs are so long and skinny, they can easily get stuck in the old skeleton. The new skeleton is soft and takes several hours to harden. If it hardens

Opposite: A South African walkingstick nymph climbs out of its old exoskeleton.

Young stick insects like this one molt up to eight times before emerging as fully grown adults.

while the nymph is stuck in the old skeleton, the nymph will die.

Each time the stick insect molts, it gets a little bigger. Nymphs molt two to eight times before they get wings and become adults. Then they look for mates and produce the next generation of stick insects.

Home in
the Trees

Stick insects live on the plants they eat. Other plant-eating insects burrow under bark or into leaves for shelter. Stick insects simply live on the leaves and bark, exposed to the rain and sun. Their movements change as day becomes night and night becomes day. During the day they hide under leaves or at the base of grass stalks. They stand perfectly still to keep

A stick insect stands perfectly still in a tree to avoid being seen.

predators from seeing them. At night stick insects move slowly over the plants that are their home, eating as they go. A single stick insect can strip the leaves off a foot of branch every day. In Australia, spur-legged phasmids have been known to strip the leaves from their eucalyptus tree homes.

Many Sticks on a Tree

Stick insects are **solitary**. They interact with other stick insects only when they mate. But they are not **territorial**, so they do not fight over space on a tree. This means that many stick insects, sometimes hundreds, can share the same plant. If each tree can house a lot of stick insects, it can add up to huge numbers of stick insects in a forest. In the forests of Michigan and Wisconsin, there are sometimes so many northern walkingsticks that the noise of their eggs and droppings falling to the ground sounds like the pattering of rain.

    Some stick insects can be found on only one type of plant. Others are less picky. In Australia, the

Stick insects have big appetites. Here, a stick insect makes a meal of a leaf.

spur-legged phasmid and Lauri's ring-barker insect live on nearly any kind of eucalyptus tree. In the midwestern United States, northern walkingsticks live mainly on black oak and sour cherry trees. The western walkingstick of Colorado is found only on the slimleaf scurfpea, a kind of wild alfalfa.

Stick insects like this Malaysian stick insect usually live alone.

Once in a while, stick insects actually destroy all the plants or trees that serve both as home and food. When that happens, the stick insects either find new homes, or die. When northern walkingsticks ate up all the black oak in a Wisconsin forest in the 1940s, red maple and pine grew in its place. Northern walkingsticks do not eat red maple leaves or pine needles. Without food, they died out in that area.

The northern walkingstick lives mainly on black oak and sour cherry trees.

Hard to Catch

Opposite: A colorful stick insect in Borneo gets ready to eat (main), while a thorny phasmid devours a leaf (inset).

All stick insects are **herbivores**. They eat only plants. Because they stand on the outside of plants, stick insects are exposed to animals that might want to eat *them*. These include ants, spiders, praying mantises, lizards, frogs, and birds. Because stick insects look like leaves and twigs, predators usually leave them alone. A stick is not nearly as tasty as a bug.

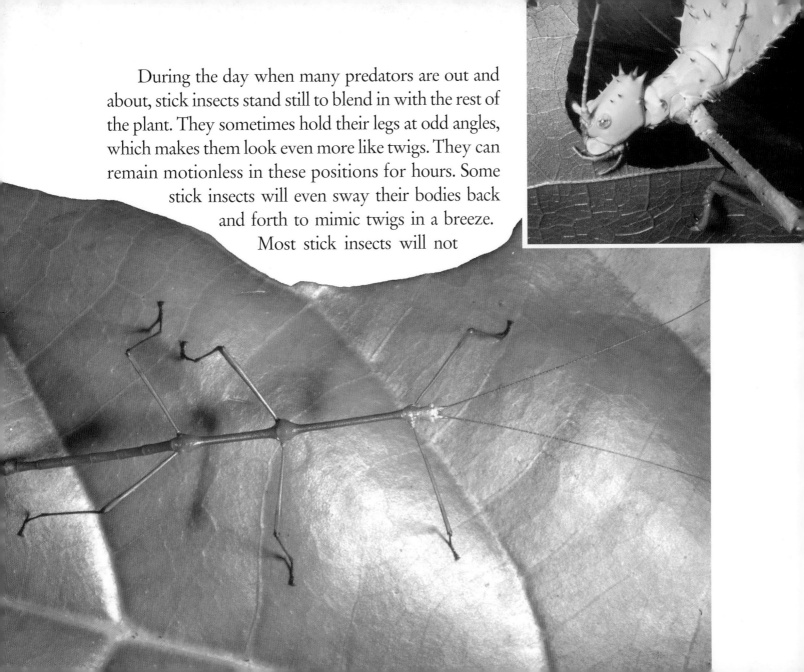

During the day when many predators are out and about, stick insects stand still to blend in with the rest of the plant. They sometimes hold their legs at odd angles, which makes them look even more like twigs. They can remain motionless in these positions for hours. Some stick insects will even sway their bodies back and forth to mimic twigs in a breeze. Most stick insects will not

Some stick insects, like this Macleay's spectre, make themselves look bigger when they feel threatened.

even move if a predator pokes them, because real sticks never crawl away.

Flight and Surprise

If the predator does not give up, stick insects have other ways of escaping. Many will drop to the ground and play dead. Some, like the Thailand winged stick insect, will jump or fly away, then stand motionless when they land. Because the insects match the background of leaves and branches, it is very hard for the predator to spot them a second time.

Some stick insects try to frighten the predator. They raise their wings to make themselves look bigger. They flash bright colors or curve their abdomen like a scorpion to look threatening. They rub their wings or antennae together to make a buzzing noise. Some stick insects can even detach a leg when grabbed by a predator. The leg keeps twitching after it comes off. This keeps the predator busy while the stick insect runs away.

Stick Weapons

A few stick insects fight back when they are attacked. Male thorn-legged stick insects from New Guinea have large spines on their legs that they can drive into a predator's skin. The spines are hard and sharp and they hurt.

Other stick insects use chemical weapons. The two-striped walkingstick from the southeastern United

The great spiny stick insect uses its spiny legs to protect itself.

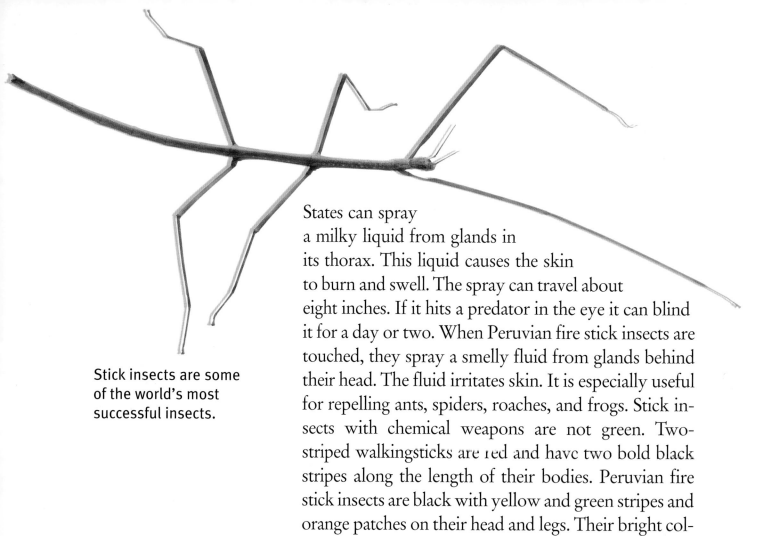

Stick insects are some of the world's most successful insects.

States can spray a milky liquid from glands in its thorax. This liquid causes the skin to burn and swell. The spray can travel about eight inches. If it hits a predator in the eye it can blind it for a day or two. When Peruvian fire stick insects are touched, they spray a smelly fluid from glands behind their head. The fluid irritates skin. It is especially useful for repelling ants, spiders, roaches, and frogs. Stick insects with chemical weapons are not green. Two-striped walkingsticks are red and have two bold black stripes along the length of their bodies. Peruvian fire stick insects are black with yellow and green stripes and orange patches on their head and legs. Their bright colors warn predators to stay away.

GLOSSARY

abdomen: The third segment of an insect's body.

antennae: Sense organs found on an insect's head. They are used to smell the insect's surroundings.

camouflage: To hide using a disguise.

capitulum: A fatty structure attached to one end of a stick insect egg in order to attract ants.

exoskeleton: A hard skeleton found on the outside of an animal.

herbivore: Any animal that eats only plants.

molt: Process of shedding an old exoskeleton in order to grow larger.

nymph: Immature insect. Resembles adult but is wingless.

operculum: The "door" on one end of a stick insect egg that a nymph pushes open when it hatches.

phasmid: The scientific name for stick insects. *Phasmid* means "ghost."

pheromone: A chemical that signals readiness for mating.

predator: Any animal that hunts and eats other animals.

solitary: Lives alone instead of in groups.

tegmina: The leathery front pair of wings on a stick insect. They protect the back pair of "flying" wings.

territorial: An animal defending an area against members of its own species.

thorax: The middle segment of an insect's body, where the legs and wings attach.

FOR FURTHER EXPLORATION

Books

Sally Stenhouse Kneidel, *Stink Bugs, Stick Insects, and Stag Beetles, and 18 More of the Strangest Insects on Earth.* New York: John Wiley & Sons, 2000. Introduces many unusual insects, including stick insects, focusing on how their adaptations help them survive. An appendix lists two biological supply companies and eleven insect zoos.

Patrick Merrick, *Walkingsticks.* Chanhassen, MN: Childs World, 1997. This book from the Naturebooks series contains close-up color photographs of stick insects along with facts about their anatomy and behavior.

Web Sites

BugBios (www.insects.org). This Web site includes close-up pictures of stick insects.

Enchanted Learning (www.enchanted learning.com). Provides a detailed diagram of stick insect anatomy.

The Phasmid Study Group (www.stick insect.org). Has information on keeping stick insects as pets, and maintains links to other pages about stick insects.

INDEX

PICTURE CREDITS

ABOUT THE AUTHOR

Diane A. Kelly decided she wanted to be a scientist when she was eight years old. As a professional biologist, she gets to spend every day learning about animals and how their bodies work. She lives in western Massachusetts with her husband, two children, and more pets than are good for her. This is her first book for children.